OBSERVED
AND
IMAGINED

Poems and Essays
by

Robert H. Deluty

GATEWAY PRESS, INC.
Baltimore, MD   2004

Please direct all correspondence and book orders to:
Robert H. Deluty
4783 Ilkley Moor Lane
Ellicott City, Maryland 21043

Library of Congress Control Number 2004104120
ISBN 0-9704201-4-5

Published by
Gateway Press, Inc.
1001 N. Calvert Street
Baltimore, MD 21202-3897

Printed in the United States of America

To
Bertha and Morris Kreppel
&
Rosa, Zev, and Hinda Dluto

Other books by Robert H. Deluty
published by Gateway Press

Within and Between (2000)
The Long and Short of It: Essays and Poems (2003)

Table of Contents

20   *Back in my day*
       fast-food restaurant
       demented father
       March morning in Maine
       library entrance

21   evoking smiles
       Siamese cat
       La Jolla bistro
       on his nightstand
       expectant father

22   fiancée staring
       another birthday
       going deaf
       twenty years later
       Monday, at dawn

23   vegan child
       ten-year-old golfer
       hyperactive son
       eight o'clock final
       after the car wash

24   ten bobblehead dolls
       human cannonball
       doctor's office wall
       Thanksgiving dinner
       teacher with cancer

25   the verdict is read
       SARS epidemic
       last play of the game
       waiting for Santa
       inner-city court

26   three-year-old walking
       teen-aged engineer
       orphaned ducklings

pregnant woman
on vacation

37 sweltering beach day
baseball bullpen
baby boomer's son
clown college grad
on the title page

38 ricocheting
high tide on the beach
teenaged patriot
mother, girlfriend
sleepless new father

39 husband, wife, daughter
matching gold studs
widower cursing
elderly hippie
husband and wife

40 summer toadstools
third-rate carnival
raising their bows
walking backwards
antacid dust

41 eight candles aflame
Niagara Falls
in the limousine
sepia photographs
first-time parents

42 Bar Mitzvah boy
at the altar
placing sugar cubes
rookie father
power outage

three-letter crossword
depressed figure
Utah vacation

53   three-year-old son
cinema course
interfaith household
neuroscientist
waiting in the shop

54   faculty senate
kings riding horses
shy sixth grader
old Jewish man
French instructor

55   checking his mailbox
department store
his ten-year-old son
in the ER
college janitor

56   teen-aged slacker
determined girl scout
their first session
in his school locker
talk-radio host

57   Yale graduation
upscale shoe store
in a new city
statewide spelling bee
twenty years wed

58   marriage counselor
asking his children
back from Paris
abusive client
her wish comes true

Observed and Imagined

Connecting, Unburdening, and Enlightening: Reflections on Poetry and Psychotherapy

My vocations are university professor and clinical psychologist; my avocation is writing poetry. I would give the same answer to "Why do you write?" as I would to "Why do you do psychotherapy?" My goals are to connect, unburden, and enlighten.

The son of an Auschwitz survivor, I grew up in a loving family living within a crime-infested section of the Bronx. Many of my relatives and neighbors were refugees from war-ravaged Eastern Europe and had been (and/or were currently) victims of physical and psychological trauma, profound loss, mental illness, and poverty. Some of my earliest memories are of stories of extraordinary cruelty and degradation; of murdered grandparents, aunts, uncles, and cousins; of "ordinary persons" who committed these murders; and of Jewish and Gentile heroes who gave their lives to save and protect others. I felt compelled to retell their stories, either orally or in writing; and, through my professional work, to strive to understand the nature of aggression, deprivation, and prejudice, and to treat their psychological consequences. A vivid memory of my father became the following poem:

77290

I remember his left arm.
Leather-tough, lightly freckled,
Thick as a fireplace log.
Culminating in short, dense fingers
With near-perfectly round nails.
Most memorable, though, was the forearm,
Damaged by five blue numbers:
His concentration camp tattoo.
A daily/nightly reminder of
Evil and martyrdom,
Faith and resilience.

(Deluty, 1993)

The stories I tell through my poems, however, are not only about trauma, loss, and their aftermath. I also share stories about the pleasures and struggles (for myself and for others) of being a spouse, a parent, a child, a sibling, a teacher, a clinician, and a human being. These stories allow me to share my feelings, thoughts, and memories; and to experience an "unburdening" when particularly painful stories are conveyed to empathic others. When these stories touch, enlighten, or inspire my readers/ listeners to reflect on and share their own thoughts, emotions, or experiences, then they, too, may feel unburdened and connected. Two poems that I am fond of sharing and discussing with my clients and students are:

Perfectionist

Anxious when working,
Guilty if shirking.
Fearing heightened expectations
When work is commendable,
Dreading disapproving gazes
For efforts lamentable.
And should perfection be achieved,
Comfort is painfully brief,
For a fall from grace is awaited,
Stifling hope of lasting relief.

(Deluty, 1995a)

Too Long in Academia

Put latest effort in
Colleague's mailbox.
Thanks for your memo,
He noted later.
It's called a poem,
I replied.

(Deluty, 1995b)

Haiku and Senryu

I particularly enjoy writing haiku and senryu, 3-lined poems that attempt to record the essence of a keenly recalled or observed moment. Traditional haiku and senryu consist of 17 Japanese "onji/sound-symbols" in phrases of 5/7/5. Since Japanese onji are not equivalent to English syllables, adaptations of haiku and senryu written in English are typically presented in three lines totaling fewer than 17 syllables (see Priebe, 1999). Whereas haiku are objective and deal with natural/seasonal events, senryu address human subjective situations and are often satiric, pathetic, or ironic (Priebe, 2000). For example,

wallet-sized photo ...
his depressed adult daughter
as a smiling child

(Deluty, 2002a)

holiday dinner ...
discussing the dead, dying
and ought-to-be-killed

(Deluty, 2002b)

another birthday ...
waitress of thirty years
serving herself

(Deluty, 2001)

first breakfast ...
newlywed complaining
his ring's too heavy

(Deluty, 2002c)

post eye surgery
upset elder tells his wife
she looks much older

(Deluty, 2002d)

five-year-old blind girl ...
her mother tries to describe
the evening's rainbow

(Deluty, 2003)

As I have discussed elsewhere (Deluty, 2002e, 2002f), there are important similarities in the creative processes and outcomes of psychotherapy and haiku/senryu poetry. These commonalities may be found in the domains of awareness/insight; genuineness; "here-and-now" experiencing; interdependence of events; humor; use of blank space; and parsimony.

Similarities Between Haiku, Senryu, and Psychotherapy

Awareness/Insight. The purpose of haiku and senryu is "an awareness beyond the intellect" (Spiess, 2000a, p. 119). Such "awareness" is similar to the "insight" that is an aim of much psychotherapy. Rogers (1942, 1951) asserted that insight was essentially an awareness of experience, a new way of perceiving. With both my therapy clients and the readers of my poetry, my goal is to assist them in perceiving people (including themselves), as well as objects, experiences, and events, in new and different ways.

Genuineness. Spiess (1999) has advised writers that haiku and senryu "should not result from idiosyncrasies but from inner genuineness" (p. 85). Genuineness (i.e., the honest expression of feelings, attitudes, or behaviors) on the part of the therapist and the client is a necessary condition for good therapy outcomes. The therapist, wrote Rogers (1966), should be "his actual self in his encounter with his client. Without façade, he openly has the feelings and attitudes that are flowing in him at the moment ... The therapist's feelings are available to him —to his awareness—and he is able to live them, to experience them in the relationship and to communicate them if they persist" (p. 185). I believe that we could easily substitute "haiku/senryu poetry" for "therapy," "poet" for "therapist," and "reader" for "client" in the prior sentences.

"Here-and-Now" Experiencing. For haiku/senryu poets, "it is always the same time: now; and it is always in the same place: here" (Spiess, 1999, p. 86). Gestalt therapists, like haiku/senryu poets, place great value

on living in "the moment" and in a state of profound, ongoing awareness. Drawing from the theory and techniques of Gestalt therapy, I strive to assist my clients in establishing better contact with their present sensations and in developing a deeper and fuller awareness of their thoughts, feelings, overt behaviors, and environments. Successful haiku/senryu writers often accomplish these very same goals.

Interdependence of Events. Haiku and senryu can reflect, typically through the "aesthetic juxtaposition of seemingly disparate entities, the interdependent relation of all phenomena ... no entity exists solely in its own right (including one's own beloved self)" (Spiess, 1999, p. 85). Likewise, I realize, and try to help my clients appreciate, that cognitions, emotions, and overt behaviors do not exist in a vacuum; rather, they are interrelated and multi-determined phenomena that can only be fully understood in their environmental (e.g., familial, societal, cultural) contexts. The haiku/senryu poet, like the psychotherapist, "unconceals, makes manifest, the heretofore hidden relation of entities with each other, and ultimately of our relations with them—and with the world" (Spiess, 2000b, p. 119).

Humor. Like many psychotherapists, practitioners of senryu often use gentle humor when addressing the absurdity, irony, and pathos of day-to-day living. In fact, the final line of a senryu often has a comic "kick," similar to the punch line of a joke. For example,

stunned fiancé—
her gown's price tag
has a comma

(Deluty, 2000a)

their long blond hair
in matching pony tails ...
father and daughter

(Deluty, 2000b)

wolf-whistler
realizing too late
it is his sister

(Deluty, 1999)

Following in the footsteps of Albert Ellis and other rational-emotive therapists, I also employ humor to help frame and challenge my clients' irrational thinking (e.g., their selective abstraction, overgeneralization, dichotomous reasoning, and "catastrophizing"); and (on occasion and when appropriate) to buffer the pain triggered by disappointment, loss, or change.

Use of Blank Space. The artistic use of blank space (which is created by non-expression) is observable in nearly all forms of Eastern art (Izutsu, 1982). Many haiku and senryu contain an ellipsis (e.g., "...") indicating non-expressed words, images, or feelings. A haiku editor once returned my submitted poems with the following helpful (and, characteristically, very terse) advice: "Don't narrate. Simply suggest." In a sense, he was asking me to do less and to allow my readers to do more. Similarly, I try to teach my clinical psychology graduate students (as well as to remind myself of) the importance of remaining silent at opportune times. By so doing, we give our clients the chance to do much of "the work" of psychotherapy (e.g., to reflect on past behavior; to uncover and examine feelings, attitudes, and beliefs).

Parsimony. Haiku and senryu writers strive to eliminate "the unnecessary so that the necessary may speak" (Spiess, 2000a, p. 119). Parsimony is a laudable goal not only for haiku/senryu poets, but also for psychotherapists. As asserted by Graziano (1975), "given alternative hypotheses about the client's functioning and predictions of the effectiveness of various therapy strategies, the 'simpler' explanations and strategies should be employed, monitored, and evaluated. This assumes that the more inclusive interventions, simultaneously involving several subsystems, will increase the chances for disruptive negative effects within the client's system" (p. 35). A haiku or senryu that hits its mark—like a worthy clinical interpretation, intervention, or report—"neither lacks anything nor has anything in excess" (Spiess, 2000b, p. 119).

Reciprocal Benefits of Writing Poetry and Practicing Therapy

Put simply, creating poetry has made me a better therapist, and practicing psychotherapy has made me a better poet. The processes of composing poems and providing therapy *both* require that I become more aware of the nature of my past and present experience; that I be more genuine with myself and in my interactions with others; that I experience life more deeply and fully in the "here-and-now," and that I appreciate the complex interrelations of events, the great value of humor and non-expression, and the importance and elegance of parsimony.

The great majority of my three-line poems are senryu. As a long-time clinical psychologist and teacher who has lived most of my life in large cities, I feel much more comfortable writing poems with intrapersonal and interpersonal themes than I do writing haiku about flora, fauna, or the seasons. In addition, my clients often provide wonderful "material" for my poetry, and senryu allow me countless opportunities to address the comic, tragic, and ironic aspects of daily life.

The discipline inherent in writing senryu has resulted in my being more observant of what goes on within and around me, and in my sharing these observations as clearly and concisely as possible with my clients. The haiku editor's admonition about "suggesting" rather than "narrating" has carried over to my clinical work; I find that I am now doing less lecturing to my clients (my undergraduate and graduate students, however, are not so fortunate). Having particular clients read and then discuss selected poems has resulted in shared smiles, tears, laughter, remembrances, insights, understanding, and healing.

Regarding Criticism

In addition to being asked questions concerning how, when, and why I write, I am frequently asked about my reactions to praise, criticism, and rejection of my poetry. Although I truly appreciate supportive and approving responses (who doesn't?), I value thoughtful, constructive criticism even more. Indifference or the absence of a response to my poetry is far more difficult for me to handle than is criticism, even if it is harsh.

There are colleagues, friends, and family members to whom I have sent batches of my published poems (some haiku/senryu, some longer pieces) every few months. A considerable number of these folks have never or very rarely offered a response. Over the course of a few years, some were sent as many as several hundred poems of different styles and topics, and had not acknowledged receiving any of them. [A very slow learner, I finally stopped sending them my poems.] I do not give people my poetry, nor do I seek its publication, in order to show off or elicit compliments. Rather, I do so because I have *felt* something, *seen* something, *heard* something, *remembered* something, or *imagined* something (a) that was meaningful to me; (b) that I was able to express in (what I hoped was) some novel or interesting way; and, most importantly, (c) that I wanted to share with others. Making a connection, evoking a smile, relieving a burden, touching a heart, promoting greater awareness, casting the familiar in a new light—this is why I write and why I share what I have written. It is also why I am a psychotherapist.

References

Deluty, R.H. (1993, November 16). 77290. *The Baltimore Sun*, 19A.

Deluty, R.H. (1995a, June 27). Perfectionist. *The Wall Street Journal*, A17.

Deluty, R.H. (1995b). Too long in academia. *The Pearl, 13*, 11.

Deluty, R.H. (1999). wolf-whistler. *Modern Haiku, 30*(3), 36.

Deluty, R.H. (2000a). stunned fiancé. *Haiku Headlines, 13*(1), 2.

Deluty, R.H. (2000b). their long blond hair. *Modern Haiku, 31*(3), 26.

Deluty, R.H. (2001). another birthday. *Haiku Headlines, 14*(6), 2.

Deluty, R.H. (2002a). wallet-sized photo. *Up Dare?, 31*, 21.

Deluty, R.H. (2002b). holiday dinner. *Modern Haiku, 33*(2), 12.

Deluty, R.H. (2002c). first breakfast. *The Pegasus Review*, January/February issue, 4.

Deluty, R.H. (2002d). post eye surgery. *winterSPIN, 43*, 5.

Deluty, R.H. (2002e). Psychotherapy and haiku/senryu poetry: Common ground. *Modern Haiku, 33*(1), 67–70.

Deluty, R.H. (2002f). West meets East: Processes and outcomes of psychotherapy and haiku/senryu poetry. *Journal of Poetry Therapy, 15*(4), 207–212.

Deluty, R.H. (2003). five-year-old blind girl. *Up Dare?, 32*, 54.

Graziano, A. M. (1975). Introduction: Behavior therapy with children. In A.M. Graziano (Ed.), *Behavior therapy with children* (Vol. II, pp. 1–36). Chicago, IL: Aldine.

Izutsu, T. (1982). *Toward a philosophy of Zen Buddhism*. Boulder, CO: Prajna Press.

Priebe, D. (1999). 11th anniversary issue feature. *Haiku Headlines, 12*(1), 8.

Priebe, D. (2000). Introduction. *Haiku Headlines, 12*(11), 1.

Rogers, C.R. (1942). *Counseling and psychotherapy: Newer concepts in practice.* Boston, MA: Houghton Mifflin.

Rogers, C.R. (1951). *Client-centered therapy: Its current practice, implications, and theory.* Boston, MA: Houghton Mifflin.

Rogers, C.R. (1966). Client-centered therapy. In S. Arieti (Ed.), *American handbook of psychiatry* (Vol. 3, pp. 183–200). New York: Basic Books.

Spiess, R. (1999). Speculations. *Modern Haiku, 30*(2), 85–86.

Spiess, R. (2000a). Speculations. *Modern Haiku, 31*(1), 119–120.

Spiess, R. (2000b). Speculations. *Modern Haiku, 31*(2), 118–119.

Originally published in Voices: The Art and Science of Psychotherapy, *2003, Volume 39, No. 3, pp. 57–62.*

renowned physician
seeks a second opinion
from his grandmother

You're doubly blessed ...
exhausted mother of twins
offers no response

elderly wife
trying to recall his smile
when they first met

school lunchroom soup
served by an angry bald man
wearing a hair net

intently watching
a deaf couple signing ...
a boy smiles and waves

struggling actor
whispering soliloquies
as he folds napkins

breaking the fast ...
baby chews a yarmulke
placed on his head

nursing home roommates
each in a demented haze ...
mother and daughter

first day of school
before the introductions
a stutterer prays

winter morning ...
a small black dog walking
an old woman

cochlear implant ...
hearing his daughter's laugh
for the first time

middle school dance ...
stick-figured preteen boys
mustering courage

dieting mother
licking the candy wrappers
in her son's lunchbox

performance artist
falls, clutching his chest ...
unsure audience

dentist's office ...
an old man asks the price
of cleaning three teeth

adopted child
unsheathes her sharpest dagger:
You're not my father

through a store window
watching *The French Chef* ...
homeless family

floating in the pool
overweight child rejoicing
in his weightlessness

adjusting her wig
in the high school bathroom ...
fifteen, on chemo

bewildered children
don't recognize the father
being eulogized

Euphemisms

More than the late morning school bus pick-ups,
And the parent-friendly homework assignments,
And even the wonderfully awful band recitals,
I will miss his teachers' disciplinary notes,
So artfully phrased and painstakingly
inoffensive:

"David had much difficulty today controlling his
enthusiasm."

"David is very anxious to share his insights with
his neighbors."

"David never misses the opportunity to find
humor in seemingly serious situations."

The eleven-year-old class clown,
Graduating to middle school,
Should be thankful for teachers who
Should have been diplomats.

blind man's wife
silently removes the hair
floating in his soup

the same nightmare—
stripped of his Ph.D.
for failing gym

their six-year-old son
at a Jackson Pollock show ...
I can drip better

visiting hours ...
their schizophrenic daughter
blaming them and God

Children's Hospital ...
at the foot of her bed
a Christmas stocking

Back in my day ...
old teacher reminisces
amidst yawns, groans

fast-food restaurant ...
rail-thin mother glaring
at obese daughter

demented father
smiles, introduces himself
to his adult son

March morning in Maine,
thirty-eight degree weather ...
collegians in shorts

library entrance ...
professors and their students
lighting cigarettes

evoking smiles
a Princeton bumper sticker
on his pick-up truck

Siamese cat
glaring at her owner ...
skim milk in her bowl

La Jolla bistro ...
Botoxed grandmothers
in halter tops

on his nightstand
a *World's Best Dad* mug
filled with bourbon

expectant father
orders another dessert ...
eating for three

fiancée staring
at his first wife's name ...
an old tattoo

another birthday,
another body piercing ...
his pained mother

going deaf
engraves into memory
his daughter's voice

twenty years later
sending his fifth grade teacher
a thank-you note

Monday, at dawn
strangers on the subway
sleeping together

vegan child
feeling guilty while eating
animal crackers

ten-year-old golfer
hurling his ball and putter
at the windmill

hyperactive son
speaking in paragraphs
in his sleep

eight o'clock final ...
a student in the front row
wearing pajamas

after the car wash
drying off his daughter
with a leaf blower

ten bobblehead dolls
jiggling near a high-speed fan ...
his son's handiwork

human cannonball ...
his parents wondering
where he'll end up

doctor's office wall ...
underneath the diplomas
his baby's footprints

Thanksgiving dinner ...
elders and toddlers dozing
before dessert

teacher with cancer
listening to her students
whine about finals

the verdict is read …
one juror begins sobbing,
another smiles

SARS epidemic …
Hong Kong ballerinas
in surgical masks

last play of the game
peering through binoculars
at a cheerleader

waiting for Santa
atop a jigsaw puzzle …
their daughter, asleep

inner-city court …
icicles hanging down
from netless hoops

three-year-old walking
with her six-foot eight father …
five steps for his one

teen-aged engineer
using a garage door
to crack walnuts

orphaned ducklings
searching along the river
for a leader

sleeping beside
a pile of clean laundry …
out-of-town spouse

a family's gift …
three generations able
to raise one eyebrow

on a metal desk
under a sea of memos
one springtime haiku

old psychiatrist
in a downtown porn shop
claiming it's research

Sikh grandfather
sporting a white turban
and red Nikes

gravely ill father
smiling from ear to ear
holds birth announcement

at the doughnut shop
requesting a bran muffin ...
rogue policeman

Memorial Day …
a John Wayne film festival
at grandfather's house

Nobel laureate
giving a keynote address,
his fly wide open

great-grandmother
painting tiny gray streaks
on her jet-black wig

a good wind …
neighbors raking my leaves
off their lawns

four-year-old daughter
styling her doll's tresses
with a new toothbrush

no pen at hand ...
her exquisite senryu
evaporating

Jewish fisherman
questioning his rabbi
about porkpie hats

Day of Atonement—
shofar blasts muffle
his hunger pangs

condemned building ...
candidates' campaign stickers
on boarded windows

college commencement ...
red-faced provost mangling
Pakistani names

déjà vu ...
his doctor's diagnosis
repeats a nightmare

for a few moments
sheds his oxygen tubes,
smokes a cigarette

walking up the aisle
toilet tissue on one heel—
oblivious groom

hysterical child ...
pet mouse's tail hanging
from neighbor cat's mouth

red stain on the road ...
a wayward young deer
two weeks ago

seventh grade boys,
first-year English teacher
look for openings

pre-game ...
baseball coach catnapping,
hands and jaw clenched

masquerade party
at the Red Cross blood bank
vampires abound

after the fall
the intrepid one-year-old
smiles, looks forward

post-Thanksgiving Day ...
saints and sinners atoning
at the health club

Pathways to Aggressive, Assertive, and Submissive Behavior

"Why is my son so aggressive?" "Why won't my daughter stand up for herself?" "Why do my children punch, kick, and scream whenever they are frustrated or angered?" Mental health professionals are routinely asked such questions by concerned parents. Although the questions are simple and straightforward, often the answers are not. Children act aggressively, assertively, or submissively for a wide variety of reasons; generally, a combination of factors underlies how a particular child will behave in any given situation. These factors include how the child sizes up the situation, what response alternatives she can think of, and what she expects will be the consequences of each response alternative.

The assertive child expresses herself openly and directly while respecting the rights and feelings of others. For example, in response to being teased about her new haircut, Sally says calmly, assertively, "Please stop teasing me. You wouldn't like it if I made fun of you. I really like the way my hair looks." If assertiveness entails both self-expression and the non-violation of others' rights, then unassertiveness can take one of two forms: aggressiveness or submissiveness. Aggressive children express their thoughts and feelings openly, but they do so coercively and at other people's expense. Submissive children take into account the feelings, power, and/or authority of others, but deny (or do not stand up for) their own rights and feelings.

For some aggressive children and for some submissive children, the thought of acting assertively simply never occurs to them. These children see their options as limited to "fight" or "flight;" for example, Tommy may think that when he is ridiculed, his only options are to punch, pinch, bite, scream, or spit ("fight" responses), or to run away, cry, hide, or sulk ("flight" responses). In Tommy's world of black and white options, shades of gray (i.e., assertive solutions) are nowhere to be found.

Other aggressive and submissive children, however, *can* conceive of assertive alternatives, but choose not to exhibit such behavior because they believe that aggressive or submissive acts will yield greater benefits and/or fewer costs than assertive behaviors. For example, James may physically threaten or verbally abuse his classmates because it results in their giving him their lunch money and doing his homework; as far as James is concerned, aggression "pays." In contrast, Patty may exhibit much submissive behavior because she believes submissive acts are kinder and more "ladylike" than aggressive or assertive responses; she may fear that assertive expression will result in unpleasant confrontation and diminished popularity (e.g., "If I let them know how I feel, they may get mad at me and no longer want to play with me"). Clearly, the consequences (real or imagined) that a child associates with particular behaviors have a powerful influence on the actions he/she chooses.

Parents play a critical role in shaping aggressive and prosocial behavior in their children. Boys (who consistently manifest more physical and verbal aggression than girls) tend to be given more freedom than girls to express aggression toward their parents and their peers; in contrast, girls receive relatively more praise for being "good" and are more often threatened with withdrawal of parental love for "bad" behavior. Non-aggressive boys have been shown by psychology researchers to be far more likely than aggressive males to have had parents who placed high demands on them to be "polite" and "responsible."

Although much behavior is shaped into new patterns by direct rewards (e.g., parental compliments) or punishments (e.g., withdrawal of privileges), social behaviors like aggressiveness or assertiveness are acquired largely through the process of imitation or modeling. A crucial determinant of a child's aggressiveness, assertiveness, and submissiveness is the interpersonal behavior exhibited by the parents, teachers, and peers who serve as models in the child's environment. Parents who rant, scream, and slam doors when things do not go their way typically do not have far to look when searching for the principal causes of their children's aggressiveness.

When teaching children how to be assertive, parents must pay careful attention to both the verbal and nonverbal components of assertiveness. Parents need to attend to not only what the child is saying, but how he/she is saying it. An assertive verbalization (e.g., "Please turn down the music. It's hurting my ears.") may be undone by a whiny, unsteady voice and poor eye contact. Furthermore, children should be taught how to be assertive not only in the face of conflict (e.g., in response to frustration, aggression, or ridicule), but also under pleasurable circumstances. Learning how to give or accept a compliment, or how to express agreement with others' opinions is at least as important as learning how to stand up for oneself in conflictual situations.

It is also important for children to understand that assertive behavior is not always the most adaptive means of handling conflict. Indeed, under certain circumstances, assertiveness would be counter-indicated. If a child is in the process of being physically attacked by a group of older, stronger kids, assertive expression ("Guys, it makes me angry when I'm punched and kicked") would likely be extremely unproductive. In some situations, submissively complying with an unreasonable request could strengthen a friendship or advance an important long-range goal. Thus, children need to be advised not only how to express themselves assertively, but also when (and when not) to do so.

Approximately 2000 years ago, the great sage, Hillel, posed the following questions: "If I am not for myself, who will be for me? And if I am only for myself, what am I? And if not now—when?" Some of the most important lessons we can teach our children involve how to balance self-expression and self-interest with concern for others and appreciation of others' rights and feelings. And when should parents teach these lessons? As Hillel asked, "If not now—when?"

Originally published as "Assertiveness vs. aggressiveness: What's the difference?" in Maryland Family Magazine, *1995, August issue, pp. 26–27.*

another loss …
eight-year-old Cubs fan
blaming himself

female CEO
slipping off her white pumps
closes the deal

his daughter's date
enters the restaurant
a toothpick dangling

pregnant woman
at her first rodeo …
the baby kicking

on vacation
circus contortionist
unwinding

sweltering beach day ...
two toddlers sit in the shade
of their wide uncle

baseball bullpen ...
a pigeon relieves itself
on an Oriole

baby boomer's son
finds a mauve Nehru jacket
in his Dad's closet

clown college grad ...
his tuxedo's carnation
squirting seltzer

on the title page
of her book-length thesis
professor writes *Good*

ricocheting
between child and adult …
senior prom dates

high tide on the beach …
two tortoise sand sculptures
slowly eroding

teenaged patriot
wearing an Old Glory thong—
July fourth evening

mother, girlfriend
seeking common ground …
their first dinner

sleepless new father
untying from his mailbox
deflated balloons

husband, wife, daughter
taking an evening stroll
each on a cell phone

matching gold studs ...
her son's right eyebrow
his girlfriend's tongue

widower cursing
last month's credit card bill ...
his wife's pedicures

elderly hippie ...
his great-grandchild tugging
pony-tailed white hair

husband and wife
shouting *Night* to each other
from their bedrooms

summer toadstools ...
umbrellas and microphones
whitening his lawn

third-rate carnival ...
beside the tattoo artist,
two cans of *Lysol*

raising their bows
fifth grade violinists
begin fencing

walking backwards
into a howling wind ...
her children giggling

antacid dust
on the passenger seat ...
driving instructor

eight candles aflame
amidst thousands of bulbs ...
their interfaith street

Niagara Falls ...
their seven-year-old son
requests a barrel

in the limousine
leaving the wedding chapel
the argument starts

sepia photographs
dating back ninety years
beside the casket

first-time parents
praying for courage, guidance ...
legless newborn

Bar Mitzvah boy
in front of the mirror
looking for the man

at the altar
wondering how she'll look
in thirty years

placing sugar cubes
between her cheek and gum
before sipping tea

rookie father
passionately debating
his two-year-old

power outage …
reading Edgar Allan Poe
by candlelight

after the breech birth
looking out the window
at a full moon

old French professor,
young Haitian janitor
swapping idioms

the groom's mother
trying not to notice
the bride flirting

perfectionist
worrying she'll disappoint
her psychiatrist

eight in the morning
master teacher takes on Kant ...
standing room only

high school curmudgeon
searching for any reason
to deny an A

Idaho ...
haiku far outnumber
the senryu

philosopher counts
the errors in their logic:
candidates debate

physics professor
pushing against a door—
its sign says Pull

haiku heretic
writing poems of two lines,
twenty syllables

grocery checkout ...
standing beside the teacher
whose class he cut

kitchen cabinet ...
spider sidling across
insecticide can

one month after
his article's acceptance
the journal folds

their son's fiancée ...
two nipple rings protruding
through her t-shirt

amused toddler ...
her hopping, screaming father
holds a broken toe

longtime widow
opens her wedding album ...
Valentine's Day

pro basketball game ...
coaches in Savile Row suits,
players in tattoos

child prodigy
explaining pension reform
to his mailman

Grammy winner ...
tears, shrieks, profanity
and thanks to Jesus

their son's articles
displayed in every room ...
immigrant parents

at the podium
bejeweled A-list actress
speaking for the poor

on her front lawn
in the February snow
an initialed heart

silently reading,
wondering what might have been—
a child's tombstone

sixtieth birthday ...
holding a high school photo
and a mirror

two professors
asking their ten-year-old son
how to reboot

haiku poet …
on his deathbed, requesting
a short eulogy

master clinician
lauded by strangers world-wide,
feeling lost at home

absent student
e-mailing her professor:
Please send me your notes

trying to compute
the calories she has burned
chewing toffee

on his resumé
among the references
his parents' names

Seize the Opportunity

Dear Students:

   Like many of you, I am a member of the first generation in my family to go to college. As a result of the Nazi invasion of Poland and the subsequent Holocaust, my father lost his parents and sister, and was deprived of even a high school education. My mother, who at the age of 14, fled with her parents from Austria, was a splendid student despite the fact that she did not know a word of English before arriving in America. All set to enroll in college, her plans were permanently de-railed by the death of her father shortly after her high school graduation, and by the need for her to find a job to support her mother.

   Denied the chance to attend college themselves, my parents did everything in their power to ensure that my brothers and I would have the educational opportunities of which they could only dream. My parents taught me that the chance to go to college was an extraordinary privilege, a gift beyond measure. *It still is.*

   Dear students, make the most of this wonderful opportunity accorded you. The playwright George Bernard Shaw once quipped that youth is wasted on the young. Every day, you should do all in your power to demonstrate that Shaw was dead wrong.

   The opposite of good is not evil, wrote Nobel Laureate Elie Wiesel. It is indifference. Dear students, do *not* be indifferent to your courses. Choose them wisely, attend them regularly, study diligently, and go beyond what is required. Do not be afraid to take a demanding class in which a high grade is not assured. Pursue both depth and breadth of knowledge. Take courses in fields about which you may know nothing—you'll be amazed how a class in, for example, art history or cultural anthropology or political philosophy will broaden, challenge, and enlighten you.

Do *not* be indifferent to your teachers. Ask questions when you are lost or unsure. *Never* feel comfortable with ignorance. Respectfully challenge your teachers when you disagree with them. Visit them during their office hours and engage them in discussion. Don't wait until the end of the semester to offer criticism or praise, and then do so only anonymously. If a teacher has given a splendid lecture or fostered an enlightening discussion or cleared up a long-held misconception, let them know of your appreciation at the conclusion of the class. Praise that is timely and deserved is valued by faculty just as much as it is by students.

Lastly, do *not* be indifferent to your fellow students or college community. If you know of a classmate who is struggling with academic or personal problems, offer some assistance—a kind word, a tutoring session, a ride to the nearest doughnut shop. Get involved in student organizations and governance. Support your fellow students by attending their theatre, dance, and music performances. Volunteer your time and energy to the community service projects that bring your school's resources to needy individuals and families.

One of my former professors once complained about some of his students going through graduate school "double-parked." He was referring to those students who only set foot on campus to take courses, and then rushed back to their cars once their classes were done. Do *not* attend college double-parked. Take full advantage of your school's academic, research, cultural, athletic, and public service opportunities. We, your teachers, are deeply committed to your personal and professional growth, and, in turn, we are confident that you will help *us* grow wiser and stronger.

We are honored and delighted to have you join our community of scholars, and we wish you all the very best!

Originally published in The Baltimore Sun, *September 5, 2003, p. 15A. The article is based on the keynote address I delivered at UMBC's Convocation on August 26, 2003.*

during surgery
doctors quizzing each other
on M*A*S*H* trivia

adoptive parents
rejoice in purchasing
their first formula

three-letter crossword
It can be quite inflated ...
Freudian is stumped

depressed figure
shuffling down the corridor ...
patient or staff?

Utah vacation ...
a poet's haiku juices
start flowing again

three-year-old son
asleep, raging with fever
dressed as Superman

cinema course ...
professor extols John Ford
to clueless students

interfaith household ...
stuffing their sons' stockings
with Chanukah gelt

neuroscientist
smiling as he contemplates
from where haiku come

waiting in the shop
for his daughter's manicure
a trucker reads *Vogue*

faculty senate …
a chemist fantasizes
starting a food fight

kings riding horses
across a checkerboard …
his son playing chess

shy sixth grader
trying to draw attention
to his four chest hairs

old Jewish man,
his longtime Italian friend
gesture knowingly

French instructor
informing a boy that *oui*
isn't pronounced *oy!*

checking his mailbox
one week post-Valentine's Day …
still hoping

department store …
men forming a support group
as their wives shop

his ten-year-old son
singing Eminem lyrics
while doing his math

in the ER …
his attempt as break-dancing
proved unsuccessful

college janitor
reading each chalkboard writing
before erasing

teen-aged slacker
in a dark suit, white shirt, tie ...
Halloween costume

determined girl scout
holding her cookies, walks past
Beware of Dog sign

their first session ...
her schizophrenic patient
sets his beard on fire

in his school locker
finding a tuna sandwich
of unknown age

talk-radio host
painting the world black and white,
demeans shades of gray

Yale graduation …
her father, husband, and sons
stand and applaud

upscale shoe store …
finding the perfect pair
she buys every shade

in a new city
he opens the *White Pages*
looks for his surname

statewide spelling bee …
parents of the finalists
are all foreign-born

twenty years wed
her father still wonders
what she sees in him

marriage counselor
suppressing the desire
to slap each spouse

asking his children
who put cheese in the toaster ...
deafening silence

back from Paris
handing his friends the postcards
he forgot to mail

abusive client
reminds the young therapist
of his own father

her wish comes true ...
new phone book has her name
atop a page

married forty years
his anniversary gift
is promptly returned

forgetful scholar ...
a pair of reading glasses
in every room

depressed vegan ...
her favorite cupcakes
contain beef fat

unaware student
plagiarizing an essay
by his professor

express lane ...
every woman before him
is writing a check

motorcyclist
dressing her two dachshunds
in black leather

hockey star holding
his one-year-old daughter ...
ten teeth between them

out-of-touch father
mistaking his teen's dress
for underwear

Yom Kippur morning ...
from the back of the temple
a small burp is heard

archeologist ...
searching through his papers
for a lost sandwich

faxing to Grandma
his straight-A report card
and a wish list

Make me an offer ...
old black-and-white TV
at a garage sale

home for Christmas
smelling his mother's fresh bread ...
all is forgiven

with a straight face
five-time mayor tells his son
crime doesn't pay

choosing an old dime
over a bright new penny ...
three-year-old scholar

actor's funeral ...
his widow notes wistfully
He lived, and I watched

a priest and rabbi
having heard all the jokes
don't enter the bar

indigestion ...
first dinner with his in-laws
they ask for a loan

old-time track star
unable to comprehend
synchronized swimming

northern lights display ...
ranking it as a wonder
just below childbirth

Winter Olympics ...
trying to scalp tickets
for curling final

drinking and driving
his sports car colliding
with a milk truck

haiku writer
keeping a golf pencil
in each pair of pants

Dad's stress test ...
asking her date to open
a stuck pickle jar

visiting Norway
Jewish man declines lutefisk:
We've suffered enough

Mother's Day gift …
her husband promises
not to cook dinner

preparing to dive
Olympian notices
a rip in her suit

quintuplets born
February twenty-ninth …
Dad ponders the odds

reunion photo …
each family member
has rabbit ears

Are my hips too big? …
grandfather turning off
his hearing aid

teacher-of-the-year
canceling three classes
to pick up her prize

his gift of roses
evoking surprise, pleasure
and suspicion

old world professor
searching throughout the college
for a blackboard

award assembly ...
a *perfect attendance* child
is out with a cold

home-ec teacher
bringing to her family
the day's leftovers

broken dishwasher ...
putting on her to-do list
to buy paper plates

teacher's note
sent back by child's father ...
misspelled words circled

after breakfast
does his daily exercise:
writing one poem

retired salesman
still shining his wingtips
every morning

explains to his wife
her being called phat
is a good thing

his old neighborhood ...
an X-rated movie house
where the Y once stood

thirteenth birthday ...
his aunt tells him the story
of his father's life

avian arrow ...
birds in a V-formation
cut through the fog

wife and four daughters
with premenstrual syndrome ...
man-of-the-year

Chinese professor
visiting Green Bay, worries
about the cheese hats

her five-year-old son
praying for healthy babies ...
pregnant pet hamster

Christian heretic
vowing to give up guilt
during Lent

depressed grandfather
refusing to take Prozac
opts for Harpo Marx

eye doctor's office ...
four-year-old boy staring
at all the pirates

ninth grade math class ...
a child seeing the beauty
of geometry

Dinner Guests

A generation ago, a popular parlor game involved asking the question, "If you were throwing a dinner party and could invite any five people from the past or present, whom would you choose?"

When I was first posed this question, I was fifteen years old and living in the Bronx, New York with my parents and two brothers. My answers were Moses, Abraham Lincoln, Babe Ruth, Lenny Bruce, and Sophia Loren. Every few years since then, I have asked myself the question and have noticed that my answers keep changing.

When I was in college and graduate school, writers (including Shakespeare, Chekhov, and Twain), innovative thinkers (such as Freud and Einstein), and national leaders (Churchill and Gandhi, in particular) dominated my lists. Over the next 15–20 years, my lists began including composers (Bach and Gershwin), singers (Enrico Caruso and Ella Fitzgerald), and artists (Michelangelo and Van Gogh).

I asked myself the question again a few days ago. I am now 49 years old. My wife (of two decades) and I have a 15-year-old daughter and an 11-year-old son. My mother is 78, and has been a widow since my father passed away in 1981. The answer I came up with surprised me, because my new dinner party list did not contain anyone famous. It consisted of my wife, my children, and my parents.

My father died far too young. He did not have the opportunity to meet my wife and children, to enjoy retirement with my mother, and to learn of the personal and professional successes of his sons, daughters-in-law, and grandchildren. Rather than invite five strangers (albeit, five very illustrious ones) to dinner, I'd much prefer to have my wife and children meet my father, and to have my parents share a meal with each other and their family.

The chance to have my wife, children, and father spend a few hours getting to know one another; the chance to hear my parents chat, laugh, and bicker once again; and the chance for me to ask my father the questions I never had the chance to pose, and to tell him how very much I loved and respected him—these are the principal reasons that, right now, I'd choose my "family five" over any renowned quintet. My bet is that, when I ask myself the question again years from now, my answer will remain the same.

Originally published in The Pegasus Review, *2004, March/April issue.*

Index of Poems' Original Sources

Many of the poems presented in *Observed and Imagined* have been published elsewhere. Listed below are the titles of these poems and the journals and periodicals in which they first appeared.

Author's Note

The son of a Polish father and Austrian mother,
Robert H. Deluty was born and raised in New York City.
He received his Ph.D. in Clinical-Community Psychology
from the State University of New York at Buffalo. Since
1980, he has been a psychology professor at the University
of Maryland, Baltimore County; in 2002, he was named
UMBC's Presidential Teaching Professor. He lives in
Ellicott City, Maryland with his wife, Barbara, and their
children, Laura and David.